Keep up with all the great adventures,
and don't miss a single experience!

WILD IN THE U.S.A.

by Jane Hammerslough

Based on the Animal Planet program
The Jeff Corwin Experience

SCHOLASTIC INC.

New York Toronto London Auckland Sydney
Mexico City New Delhi Hong Kong Buenos Aires

ISBN 0-439-43567-6

12 11 10 9 8 7 6 5 4 3 2   3 4 5 6 7 8/0

Printed in the U.S.A.
First printing, May 2003

Table of Contents

If you find any words that you don't understand, be sure to check out the Glossary on page 65 for help.

Q uick — name the continent that has every kind of habitat from tropics to tundra. Give up? It's North America. In fact, North America's incredible range of natural habitats is home to an awesome array of wildlife.

Made up of the United States, Canada, and Mexico, North America is a vast, varied continent. There are southern seashores that are hot and sunny year-round, while the north has many areas of permafrost, and then there are arid deserts and humid, swampy regions. In short, North America contains a range of ecosystems found nowhere else in the world — and a large variety of animals that have adapted ingeniously to these very different environments.

North America boasts a host of animals built on a large scale. Take the 8-foot-long purple snake that dwells in the Arizona desert, or the big black bears that live in Louisiana bayous. And consider the massive

Alaskan moose, the giant Pacific octopuses, and the manatees that frolic on the Florida coast, all of which are *seriously* big.

While the continent has some huge animals, it is also home to some that are small but equally fascinating, like the tough, furry little pika that lives in rocky near-Arctic regions, nectar-sipping bats, a rabbit that swims beautifully, and a spike-covered lizard that looks just like a miniature dinosaur.

If you are interested in encountering some of these amazing animals yourself, you're in luck, thanks to *The Jeff Corwin Experience*. When you join Jeff as he explores some of the most fascinating places in North America, you'll meet these animals — plus a lot more incredible wildlife.

Best of all, your ticket to this awesome journey is right in your hands.

But before we take off, some information. Jeff's trek through North America begins in the swamps and bayous of Louisiana, land of armadillos, opossums, and other incredible animals. Next stop? Arizona, home of many tough animals, including a true American original, the rattlesnake.

We'll leave the deserts of the American West and head north to Alaska, where animals such as huge musk oxen have adapted to extreme climates. Finally, we'll make our way back down south to sunny Florida, where alligators and other cool animals abound.

If you're up for venturing through swamps, across deserts, up mountains, and along some amazing coastline, you are definitely in the right place. Sit back, relax, and join Jeff on a journey through the natural world of North America.

Experience **Louisiana**

Statehood: April 3, 1812, the 18th state.

State capital: Baton Rouge, the capital since 1882.

Area: 47,717 square miles.

Elevation: The highest point is Driskell Mountain, 535 feet above sea level.

Population: 4,468,976 people, with 68 percent living in urban areas and 32 percent in rural ones.

Chief Products: Agriculture — cotton, chicken, rice, sugarcane, beef cattle, soybeans, milk. Manufacturing — chemicals, petroleum products, food products, paper products, transportation equipment. Mining — natural gas, petroleum.

The southern state of Louisiana is the birthplace of jazz music, spicy Cajun cooking, and Creole tradition and history. Louisiana's rich past meets the present in its natural history and habitats. Its swamps and bayous are still filled with fascinating animals, including armored armadillos, large black bears, unusual raptors, supershy rodents, and the only marsupial found in North America.

Armored Armadillos

Just 25 miles outside of Louisiana's vibrant capital of New Orleans, Jeff encountered an unusual animal. It was about the size of a cat, covered with tough plates,

Experience Extra: Louisiana's Atchafalaya Basin

The Atchafalaya Basin covers more than 70 miles of south-central Louisiana. It's where the floodwaters of more than 35 states flow together. The watery wilderness of the Atchafalaya Basin is a continually changing maze of bayous, streams, and lakes and is home to a diverse array of animals.

and had a long, keen nose like an anteater's. The weird-looking animal might have looked like something straight out of prehistory — but actually, it was a nine-banded armadillo.

6

Science Note

• Nine-banded armadillos are 15 to 17 inches long and weigh between 8 and 17 pounds. Originally native to South America, they now live in North American states including Texas (where they are the state animal), Oklahoma, and Kansas, as well as Louisiana.

• Armadillos eat insects, worms, termites, and other invertebrates. Their sharp nails help them dig for prey underground and in rotting wood, and their long, sticky tongues help them catch and eat their prey.

• Although armadillos have poor eyesight, they have excellent hearing and a great sense of smell.

• Excellent swimmers, armadillos inflate their intestines with air to keep their heavy-shelled bodies afloat. The animals can hold their breath for four to six minutes.

• Armadillos spend most of the day in underground burrows and hunt at night.

Nine-banded armadillos are the only animals that always give birth to four identical babies at a time. Baby armadillos are born with skin that consists of soft plates. At first, these plates are like fingernails arranged in flexible rows all over the animal. As armadillos grow, however, these plates get hard and bony. This tough, armorlike covering gives armadillos excellent protection from predators.

7

**Experience Extra:
Pop Quiz!**

When threatened, some armadillos roll themselves into a hard, protective ball. True or false?

(True!)

Louisiana Black Bears

The Louisiana black bear became the state's official mammal in 1992. Jeff and a couple of wildlife biologists who work with the animals got to experience this species of American black bear up close and personal.

But first, they had to lure the bear into a culvert

8

Science Note

• Female Louisiana black bears weigh between 120 and 275 pounds; adult males weigh between 250 and 400 pounds and can grow to 4 feet at the shoulder or about 6 feet from head to toe.

• Louisiana black bears have dense black fur and a distinctive white streak on their chests.

• Some Louisiana black bears live in trees.

• Louisiana black bears eat berries, acorns, honey, and crops such as corn, oats, wheat, and sugarcane. Although they are shy and avoid humans, the bears also eat human garbage.

• The animals have a life span of 15 to 18 years.

trap. The bait? Doughnuts!

When they found a female Louisiana black bear in their trap, the research biologists used a blow dart to tranquilize the animal with drugs so they could examine her. The bear went to sleep temporarily, and the scientists and Jeff were able to look at her teeth and claws and even touch her. This is definitely not something anyone should attempt under normal circumstances.

Because the bear's teeth were very worn down with use, the scientists and Jeff determined that she was about 15 years old. The animal's claws were dirty and stained, indicating that she had been stepping on

Experience Extra:
What's That Smell?

As Jeff discovered by closely examining the sleeping bear, Louisiana black bears have a distinctive scent. They smell just like dried milk!

berries. The scientists worked fast to measure the bear and collect other information, because after about an hour, she began to wake up.

Barred Owls

Barred owls are large birds of prey, among the largest of all raptors. They stand more than 2 feet tall and have

JEFF'S JOURNAL
ON THE BARRED OWL'S EYES

"Amazing birds. Her eyes are extraordinary. They have amazing vision. These eyes are excellent for spotting prey at night. The price she pays for having such good eyesight and having such large eyeballs is that she can't individually move her eyeballs. Instead she relies on the very extensive rotation of her head to spot prey."

a wingspan of about 50 inches. Excellent hunters, these big, beautiful birds are native to North America.

Jeff met a barred owl with a hurt wing that was part of a rehabilitation and release program. The pro-

Science Note

• Barred owls live in swamps, moist woodlands, and along riverbanks. The birds have adapted to living near humans and can even be found near cities.

• Barred owls eat mice and other small mammals, amphibians, reptiles, insects, fish, and small birds.

• Like all owls, barred owls have excellent eyesight, keen hearing, and special fringed wings that enable them to fly silently.

• Barred owls have many calls, including a hoot that sounds like a person saying, "Who cooks for you? Who cooks for you all?"

gram helps birds get enough to eat while they are healing. Once the bird is well (in this case, once its wing had healed), it can return to the Louisiana swampland.

Experience Extra:
Pop Quiz!

Because of special bones in their necks, owls can turn their heads 360 degrees around. True or false?

(False! However, owls can turn their heads an amazing 270 degrees around because of special bones in their necks!)

Swamp Rabbits

Also called cane-cutters, cane jakes, and water rabbits, swamp rabbits are never found far from water. In fact, these animals have adapted to their environments with a special talent: They're excellent swimmers.

13

Science Note

• Male and female adult swamp rabbits are about the same size, weighing as much as 6 pounds. They have dark gray or yellow-brown fur, rounded ears, and a rust-colored ring around their eyes.

• Swamp rabbits eat whatever vegetation is available, from grass to twigs and bark. They are active at night, or nocturnal, and sleep during the day.

• The animals live in hollow logs and under brush or in thickets.

• Swamp rabbits are extremely fast runners. They run in a zigzag pattern.

• To escape predators, swamp rabbits dive into water and swim. To camouflage themselves in water, they lie motionless, with only their noses visible above the water's surface.

Although swamp rabbits are not an endangered species, they are very secretive, hiding when humans are around. If you're lucky, however, you might catch a glimpse of one swimming in a floodplain, river, lake border, or other wet area.

North America's Own Marsupial

When you think of the group of animals called marsupials, Australian mammals such as kangaroos, koalas, wombats, and wallabies probably come to mind. But did you know that North America has its very own, true marsupial?

It is one of the oldest, most primitive mammals of all time. Introducing: the opossum. Opossums can be found all the way from Ontario, Canada, to South America, but they share some characteristics with their Australian relatives.

Like all female marsupials, opossums have abdominal pouches where babies continue to grow and develop after birth. The mother opossum can close her pouch to prevent her babies from falling out.

Of course, you can't visit Louisiana without getting a look at one of Louisiana's most famous animals: the alligator. Jeff went looking for alligators and found

**Experience Extra:
Pop Quiz!**
The expression "playing possum"
comes from the animal's way of
lying limp and still — acting as if
it were dead — when threatened
by predators. True or False?

(True!)

some big ones in a wildlife sanctuary. Located in the swampland, the sanctuary is carefully protected, and hunting, fishing, and trapping are strictly banned. This makes the area a perfect place for animals to live and flourish. Among the animals living in the swamp are huge alligators. These alligators can reach up to 15 feet in length, weigh as much as 1,500 pounds, and can live to be over 100 years old. But the truly amazing

Science Note

• When opossums are born, they are smaller than your fingernail. Full-grown opossums grow to be 40 inches long and weigh between 4 and 12 pounds.

• Opossums have 50 teeth, more than any other North American mammal.

• Although it is clumsy when walking on the ground, an opossum's long, scaly, prehensile (grasping) tail, long toes, sharp claws, and hand-over-hand movement make it an agile climber.

• Opossums' predators are foxes, bobcats, hawks, and owls. Nocturnal animals, opossums eat invertebrates, reptiles, insects, birds, eggs, berries, mushrooms, plants, and carrion.

• The animals do not build burrows. Instead they live in rock crevices, tree cavities, abandoned woodchuck burrows, and other dens. They move from one burrow to the next each day.

thing about these animals? In spite of their enormous size, they are almost totally invisible unless you know exactly where to look. Alligators can blend into their surroundings with remarkable ease. Except when they come out to lie on the bank and sun themselves, they spend most of their time in the water, with only their eyes and the top of their snouts sticking up out of the water. Their dark coloration blends in perfectly with the surrounding swamp and they can move incredibly quietly through the water. But we'll learn more about these reptiles when we head to Florida.

It's been fun sloshing around the swamps and bayous of Louisiana and meeting the intriguing animals that thrive in and around the water. But how about exploring a *drier* side of North America? Next stop, the blazing deserts of Arizona, home to rattling reptiles and other amazing animals.

Experience Arizona

Statehood: February 14, 1912, the 48th state.

State capital: Phoenix, the capital since 1889.

Area: 114,007 square miles.

Elevation: The highest point is Humphreys Peak, 12,633 feet above sea level.

Population: 5,130,632 people, with 87 percent living in urban areas and 13 percent in rural ones.

Chief Products: Agriculture — beef cattle, cotton, lettuce, melons, milk. Manufacturing — computer components, transportation equipment, chemicals, fabricated metal products. Mining — copper, gold.

Chapter Two:
Arizona

Survival in the Arizona desert means adapting to incredible extremes, from weathering the scorching-hot midday sun to making it through freezing winter evenings. As a result, arid Arizona is home to animals built to meet the challenges of their environment. These include toads that dig underground, bats that feed on cacti, and a host of incredibly tough reptiles — large and small.

Couch's Spadefoot Toads

Who wins the title for toughest amphibian living on the planet — or at least in North America? According to Jeff, the winner is the Couch's spadefoot toad, found in the southwestern United States.

Experience Extra:
About Arizona

In the Arizona desert, the sun shines for months, with droughtlike conditions and temperatures climbing to 110 degrees Fahrenheit or more. But suddenly, as winter approaches, the rainy season comes, bringing near-floodlike conditions. Not only must animals in the desert adapt to extremes of hot and cold, but they must also be able to survive both of the seasonal extremes.

The spadefoot toad has a hard, bony plate on its heels that looks like a little black shovel. This tough, built-in "spade" enables the toad to dig down underground

Science Note

• The Couch's spadefoot toad is about 3 inches long, the largest species of spadefoot toad.

• The toads are green, brown, or black, with small warts covering their skin, which cause sneezing in some people when they touch Couch's spadefoot toads.

• Unlike other toads that have horizontal pupils, the Couch's spadefoot toad has eyes with pupils that are vertical slits in bright light.

• Couch's spadefoot toads have a call that is similar to the sound of a bleating goat or sheep.

• The toads are nocturnal and emerge above ground only during the rainy season, when they lay eggs.

and out of the sun, where it spends most of its life.

Desert Bats

Later, Jeff met up with a scientist named Katie Hinman, and they set out at night to study bats. To capture the bats, Katie and Jeff used a mist net — a very fine net that was originally used to catch birds. After a while, they caught two different species of Arizona's nectar-eating flying mammals, the long-nosed bat and the long-tongued bat.

After observing the bats, Katie gave one a drink of sugar water, which the long-tongued bat lapped

JEFF'S JOURNAL
ON THE STRANGE LIFE OF AN UNDERGROUND TOAD

"Throughout much of the year, this creature spends his life underground. And he's only active a few weeks out of the year, and that's when the rains are at their heaviest, during the rainy season. So when this creature is underground, it doesn't need any water, because he becomes his own canteen. Some scientists speculate that a spadefoot toad can stay under the ground for a number of years, perhaps two years or more."

up. Katie gave the drink to the bat to help minimize any stress the animal might have been suffering after being caught and examined. Stress can cause animals to burn a lot of energy, leaving them vulnerable to predators.

Science Note

• These bats are both medium-sized, with wingspans between 13 and 16 inches wide. Each feeds on the nectar and pollen of desert plants such as the agave and saguaro cactus.

• Moving like hummingbirds from plant to plant to collect food, these bats play an important part in transferring pollen in night-blooming desert plant species.

• Both long-nosed and long-tongued bats have prominent, long noses and an excellent sense of smell, which helps them find and reach food.

• Long-tongued bats have tongues that are about one-third the length of their bodies.

• These nocturnal animals roost in caves.

The sugar water helps to restore energy — and Katie admitted that it was fun to watch the bat drink using its long tongue. After its energy drink, the long-nosed bat was released and resumed looking for food.

Experience Extra:
Pop Quiz!

The long-nosed bat has the longest nose of the nectar-eating bats of Arizona. True or false?

(False! The long-tongued bat actually has a longer nose than the long-nosed bat species!)

Snakes Alive!

Arizona is home to a wide variety of serpents, including the Arizona mountain king snake, gopher snakes, and rattlesnakes. Jeff says that for herpetologists (scientists who study snakes), looking for snakes in Arizona is "the ultimate treasure hunt."

Arizona Mountain King Snake

The slender body and vivid red, yellow, and black bands on the Arizona mountain king snake make it beautiful — and make it look just like the coral snake. The difference between the two serpents? While coral snakes are some of the most venomous and dangerous in North America, the Arizona mountain king snake isn't harmful to humans.

The coloration of the animal is called aposematic, meaning a sign of danger to others. However, as Jeff explains, the colors of the Arizona mountain king snake are a way of fooling other animals — and protecting the snake.

The Amazing Long-Nosed Snake

The Arizona long-nosed snake is a remarkable-looking reptile for a couple of reasons. First of all, it is very colorful with a cream-colored body with black and red or pink splotches. In addition, this type of snake has a very long nose — for a snake. But that long, pointed nose isn't

26

just for looks. It's actually an extremely useful tool that enables the snake to hunt for its favorite foods, such as small rodents, lizards and their eggs, and even small snakes. The snake can push its way into the nests or burrows of these animals by using its nose as a hoe. And during the day, the long-nosed snake can use its nose to burrow between rocks or underground, where it can hide from the sun, predators, and humans.

27

Science Note

- Also known as the Sonoran mountain king snake and the pyro, Arizona mountain king snakes are usually shorter than 42 inches and live in mountains or rock piles, coming out only to feed, mate, or find a new home.

- The snakes eat lizards, other snakes, rodents, and birds, attacking their prey by grabbing and constricting.

- Although their fangs do not deliver venom, when threatened, Arizona mountain king snakes produce a musky scent and may bite.

- The animals usually stay on the ground but are able to climb trees.

Gopher Snakes

The gopher snake that Jeff observed was big, long, and had a really loud hiss that sounded like a rattlesnake — but it is harmless to humans. This slow-moving *Colubrid* is common in the American Southwest, and its range extends into the central part of the United States. These snakes grow anywhere from 3 to 8 feet long, and they have an unusual way of fighting. When two male gopher snakes battle over territory, they wrap themselves around each other on the ground, almost like they are wrestling.

Rattlesnakes

Characterized by diamond-shaped heads, a distinctive set of rattles in their tails, and very powerful venom, rattlesnakes are a fascinating part of the Arizona landscape.

Science Note

• With an excellent sense of smell, gopher snakes hunt small rodents, lizards, birds, and other snakes.

• To fool predators into thinking they are more dangerous than they really are, gopher snakes spread and flatten their heads, vibrate their tails, and make rattling sounds to resemble rattlesnakes.

• Female gopher snakes produce up to 24 eggs at a time.

• To avoid intense heat, the snakes are nocturnal in the summer; to gather heat on rocks during cooler months, they are active during the day.

The rattles on a rattlesnake grow one segment at a time, when the snake sheds its skin each year. The older the snake, the more rattles it has. Rattles are made of keratin, the same material found in human fingernails.

Experience Extra:
Milking Mojave
Rattlesnakes!

The Mojave rattlesnake is the most poisonous of all rattlers, with venom that attacks both nerves and tissues. Combating the deadly bites of these and other poisonous snakes means creating antivenin. How do you create antivenin? With venom. In Arizona, Jeff helped Barney Tomberlin, a wildlife biologist who "milks" Mojave rattlesnakes. He collects their venom, dehydrates it, and then sends it to a laboratory to create antivenin.

Science Note

• Rattlesnakes make noise with tail rattles by vibrating them — like a person shaking a rattle. Although most of them shake their rattles as a warning to possible predators, some use soft rattling to lure curious prey.

• Rattlesnakes eat rodents, birds, lizards, and other small animals.

• Rattlesnakes belong to a family of snakes called pit vipers. Pits on the serpents' faces enable them to sense heat — and find warm-blooded prey.

• Some rattlesnakes can swim, holding their rattles above water to keep them dry.

Horned Toads in Arizona

What's a horned toad? Well, for starters, it isn't a real toad at all.

Horned toads are actually very well-camouflaged, fast-moving lizards that can be found in southeastern Arizona and other parts of the southwestern United States. To make things even more confusing, the horned toad is sometimes called a Texas horned lizard.

The horned toad is a shy animal. However, with two spiky horns on its head and rows of sharp spines that run the length of its back, it looks amazingly fierce.

31

Science Note

• Closely related to iguanas, Texas horned lizards grow to be about 7 inches long.

• Like toads, these animals have sticky tongues that they use to catch and eat ants and insects.

• Texas horned lizards come out of their burrows at sunrise and bask in the sun to raise their body temperatures. During the hottest times of day, they return to shaded areas to avoid overheating.

• When disturbed, these animals freeze in place to blend in with their surroundings, hiss, and inflate their bodies to make themselves look bigger and more threatening.

And to look *really* scary when it is threatened, it can squirt blood from its eyes!

Next up is a completely different environment and experience — this time, in the far north of North America. The Alaskan wilderness is the spectacular setting for some rare, incredible animals, including the mighty musk ox and moose.

JEFF'S JOURNAL
WHY THE HORNED TOAD IS LOW TO THE GROUND

"Number one, when he is lying out there, he's absorbing heat energy. More surface area means more heat to be absorbed by the body. Number two, it's an excellent defense. Let's say a hognose snake was coming by ... and he starts to try to swallow this animal. The toad will puff up. And the combination of making himself very large ... with those spiky thorns, those projections ... makes him a very difficult animal to swallow."

Experience Alaska

Statehood: January 3, 1959, the 49th state.

State capital: Juneau, the capital since 1900.

Area: 587,878 square miles.

Elevation: The highest point is Mount McKinley, 20,320 feet above sea level.

Population: 626,932 people, with 67 percent living in urban areas and 33 percent in rural ones.

Chief Products: Fishing — cod, crab, flounder, salmon. Manufacturing — food products, petroleum products. Mining — petroleum, natural gas, gold, silver, zinc.

Chapter Three

Alaska

With huge, wide-open spaces, Alaska is twice the size of Texas and is the only state with more square miles than people. Called "the last frontier," the vast, undeveloped wilderness of Alaska is home to some of North America's biggest and most fascinating animals, including the bull moose, the giant Pacific octopus, the massive musk ox, and the largest of all the sea lions, as well as the pika, one of the smallest, but toughest, Arctic animals.

Magnificent Moose

Moose are the largest members of the deer family, and giant Alaskan moose are the biggest of all moose species. Taller at the shoulder than a horse, and with a rack of spiky antlers that spans up to 70 inches from tip

Experience Extra:
About Alaska

When you think Alaska, think BIG. The largest state in the United States, Alaska is about 588,000 square miles, with three million lakes and 33,000 miles of coastline — 50 percent more coastline than all the other 49 states combined! Home of Mount Denali, which, at over 20,000 feet, is North America's tallest mountain, Alaska can also claim more than half of the world's glaciers.

to tip, the Alaskan bull moose is one of the most powerful animals in the Alaskan wilderness.

Bull moose grow new antlers each spring. When they start to grow, antlers are soft, have blood vessels, and are covered with velvety skin. By early fall, the moose rubs the velvety covering off on tree trunks, and the antlers have grown large, hard, and bony.

Science Note

- Adult Alaskan moose weigh between 1,000 and 1,600 pounds.

- Moose have massive, muscular bodies, long, slender legs, and cloven hooves. They are very fast runners, able to charge at 30 miles per hour.

- Although they have poor eyesight, moose have excellent hearing and a keen sense of smell, which helps them sense predators such as wolves, cougars, wolverines, bears, and humans.

- Moose live in rocky wooded areas; they eat shrubs, trees, and plants.

- Moose are good swimmers and can go underwater to escape biting mosquitoes and other insects in the summer.

An Intelligent Octopus

The giant Pacific octopus measures about 16 feet from arm to arm, making it one of the largest of all members of the octopus family. But did you know that the animal is also extremely intelligent? It's true. In experiments, scientists have found that the giant Pacific octopus can quickly solve mazes and unscrew jars to retrieve food!

Science Note

• The giant Pacific octopus has four pairs of arms with rows of suction disks that the animal uses to catch prey. Its large head contains all the animal's organs, eyes, and beaklike mouth.

• On average, this species weighs between 50 and 90 pounds, though the largest ever recorded was 600 pounds. At birth, the animal is the size of a grain of rice.

• To move quickly, the animal propels itself by forcing water out of its body.

• The giant Pacific octopus lives in rocky coastal areas ranging from California up to Alaska.

JEFF'S JOURNAL
ON OCTOPUS SHOOTING OUT WATER
FOR "JET PROPULSION"

"They've got siphons. A siphon is a large, pulsating valve along the side of its big, domelike head, and it can actually use that as a way to propel itself like a jet."

Jeff and armadillo

Manatee

Mountain king snake

Sea lion

Rattlesnake

Musk ox

Caribou

Jeff and a lizard

Pika

Water moccasin

Moose

Florida panther

Alligator

Octopus

Crocodile

Normally light brown, the giant Pacific octopus is able to change color to camouflage itself when hunting shrimp, crabs, scallops, fish, or other prey or when it is threatened. If attacked, it shoots ink at its predator.

Musk Ox

With long hair and a dense underlayer of fur called qiviut, the huge musk ox is well equipped to survive harsh winters on the Arctic tundra. Both males and females have horns, but males have a gland under their eyes that leaves a heavy musk scent when they rub against trees or bushes. This is why they are called musk oxen.

When competing with one another for mates, male musk oxen become extremely aggressive. During the mating season — called the rutting season — the males battle, ramming each other with their horns. The animals' huge neck muscles work like springs, absorbing the shock of smashing against a competitor!

39

Experience Extra:
Pop Quiz!

During the late 1800s, musk oxen were hunted to near extinction. True or false?

(True! Today, the animals Jeff met are part of a conservation effort and raised for their hair, which is made into yarn.)

Experience Extra:
Pop Quiz!

Animals that have hooves are called ungulates. True or false?

(True! Can you think of any other ungulates?)

Science Note

• Musk oxen weigh upward of 1,000 pounds and are between 4 and 5 feet tall at the shoulder. Males are larger than females.

• The animals have long, distinctive horns that grow downward, turning up at the tips. They have a hump on their backs, large neck muscles, and hard hooves that they use to break up ice to drink water in the winter.

• Musk oxen are herbivores, grazing on grass, leaves, and flowers. Like cows, they have divided, or ruminant, stomachs.

• Musk oxen travel in herds. When threatened, the animals form a circle around their young, horns facing out.

A Caribou or Two

Alaska is home to another member of the deer family — the caribou. Caribou are smaller than moose, but just

41

Science Note

- Caribou can weight between 132 and 700 pounds. Males are much bigger than females.

- They have thick coats with a dense undercoat that helps them stay warm in cold weather.

- Both males and females have antlers, which they shed each year and regrow.

- Like their relatives the moose, caribou have poor eyesight but an excellent sense of smell.

- Caribou are herbivores. They eat leaves, lichens, evergreen leaves, and will even eat small twigs.

- Caribou are very fast runners. They can reach speeds of 40 to 50 miles per hour.

like their bigger relatives, they are perfectly adapted to life on the frozen tundra.

Caribou are found in Alaska, Canada, Scandinavia, and Russia. They live in groups of anywhere from 10 to 1,000 individuals, but every year these groups form huge herds with as many as 200,000 caribou. Then, before the weather starts to get really cold, these huge herds of caribou will migrate across the plains looking for food and warmer weather. In fact, caribou can travel as much as 800 miles a year to find a better place to spend the winter.

Science Note

- At birth, Steller sea lions weigh 50 pounds and are about 4 feet long. By the time they reach adulthood, males are about 12 feet long and 1,500 pounds; females weigh 800 to 900 pounds and are between 8 and 9 feet long.

- Steller sea lions, like seals, are members of a mammal family called pinnipeds, which means "feather-footed." Pinnipeds have finlike feet that help the animals propel themselves forward.

- Sea lions have external ears that they can close when entering water. (Seals do not have external ears.)

- Like other sea lions, Steller sea lions have four weblike flippers that they use to swim the breaststroke. They can go up to 17 miles per hour in the water and can remain underwater for about five minutes at a time.

- The animals are carnivores, eating fish, small sharks, squid, and other marine animals.

Steller Sea Lions

Also called northern sea lions, Steller sea lions are the largest of all sea lions. Steller sea lions are mammals and live in herds of 200 or more animals on rocky islands along the Alaskan coastline. Unlike California sea lions that bark to communicate, Steller sea lions *growl*.

A Peek at the Pika

Alaska is home to some incredible animals on a much smaller scale also. Take the tough little pika, a mammal related to the rabbit and that lives in high-altitude, rocky areas like Alaska's Denali National Park, home of the tallest mountain in North America. This small, furry animal has adapted beautifully to survive bitter cold, high winds, and long winters in one of the harshest environments on the planet.

The color of pikas depends on where they live. In Denali, they are a shade of gray that helps them blend in with their rocky environment. In other places, their fur is a reddish or light brown shade that matches their surroundings.

A land of incredible beauty and extremes, Alaska is where daylight — or night — can last more than *20 hours* at certain times of the year. It's where temperatures regularly dip far, far below zero — and where super-

Science Note

- With large snouts and short round ears, pikas resemble guinea pigs. They are sometimes called mouse hares, rock rabbits, haymakers, or whistling hares, for the high-pitched sound they make when threatened.

- Pikas are herbivores that live in large groups in rocky burrows. During warm months, pikas collect food that is stored in a large pile that looks like a haystack outside the nest. In the winter, they transport food to the nest via an underground tunnel.

- The animals are excellent runners and jumpers, which helps them escape from predators such as wolverines, foxes, and large birds.

- Pikas give birth to four young at a time.

plentiful summer sunshine produces cabbages that weigh 300 pounds. From huge moose to tiny pikas, the animals of Alaska are an incredible testament to adaptation.

But let's just say that the animals in Alaska got tired of the winter ice and snow and could take off like humans for a holiday elsewhere in North America. Where do you think they would go?

A good guess would be our next stop, the most popular vacation destination in North America. Sit back and relax, because we're about to explore the animals of a totally different climate, this time in sunny Florida.

JEFF'S JOURNAL
ON HARDWORKING PIKAS

"What's neat about the pika is that he is going to take everything he harvests, everything he forages, and he's going to pile it into a cache. It will be made up of nuts, seeds, grass, and he'll live on that. He is not going to be hibernating at all. He is going to be active, and this cache can be anywhere from 12 to 15 pounds. And this guy weighs less than a can of soda!"

Experience Florida

Statehood: March 3, 1845, the 27th state.

State capital: Tallahassee, the capital since 1824.

Area: 58,681 square miles.

Elevation: The highest point is 345 feet above sea level in Walton County.

Population: 15,982,378 people, with 85 percent living in urban areas and 15 percent in rural ones.

Chief Products: Agriculture — oranges, tomatoes, greenhouse and nursery products, sugarcane, beef cattle. Manufacturing — food products, electrical equipment, printed materials, scientific instruments, transportation equipment, chemicals. Mining — phosphate rock.

Chapter Four:
Florida

Hundreds of years ago, Spanish explorers came to Florida in search of gold and a magical fountain of youth. Although they never discovered either of those, they *did* find plenty of other tropical treasures that survive in the Sunshine State to this day. With enormous manatees, small skinks, incredible snakes, alligators, and panthers found only in Florida, the state features a tremendous wealth of wildlife.

Is It a Mermaid — or a Manatee?

When Christopher Columbus sailed to the New World, his crew sighted mermaids swimming in the water! At least that's what they thought they were. In fact, what they saw were some of the largest and most fascinating

Experience Extra:
About Florida

Spanish explorers named Florida in the 1500s and it became a state in 1845, but people have lived there for at least 12,000 years. The rich natural resources of the area — from the thousands of miles of coastline to inland swamps — have beautifully supported both humans and a variety of animals for a long time. Although the saber-toothed tigers, mastodons, and giant armadillos that once roamed Florida are now extinct, several animal species from the distant past still live in the state.

49

marine mammals around — a distant relative of elephants called the manatee, or sea cow.

Manatees have prehensile lips that function like an elephant's trunk. They can use their mouths to grasp and pull food in.

Science Note

• Adult manatees are 10 to 13 feet long and weigh between 1,200 and 3,500 pounds. Their bodies are football-shaped, with a paddlelike tail and two short limbs that have three or four fingernails.

• Manatees live in coastal areas of Florida. They are herbivores that feed on plants in rivers, bays, and coves.

• As the animal's teeth in the front of its mouth wear down, other teeth from the rear of the manatee's mouth migrate forward as replacements. These are called marching teeth.

• Manatees have good hearing and eyesight and are able to see colors. They communicate by chirps, squeaks, and whistles.

• The animals migrate each year, seeking warm freshwater as seasons change.

A Snake, Not a Shoe

What is long, brown, looks and feels leathery, and is found in Florida? Add "highly venomous animal" and "Florida" to the description and the answer is the Florida water moccasin, one of North America's most poisonous serpents.

Florida water moccasins look slightly different from cottonmouths found elsewhere. The contrasting bands on the Florida water moccasin are easier to see than on other members of the species. Their distinctive coloring helps camouflage the animals in the damp, lush areas of Florida.

Science Note

• Related to the copperhead, the water moccasin is a pit viper and is between 3 and 6 feet long. It is also called the cottonmouth snake, for the wide, white interior of its mouth, which serves as a visible warning to other animals when the snake is agitated.

• Water moccasins live in swamps, ponds, and other damp areas. Good climbers, the snakes often hang from branches over water.

• The serpent eats rodents, reptiles, and amphibians. Like other pit vipers, it detects warm-blooded prey with a special heat-sensing organ.

• Water moccasins are aggressive snakes believed to be capable of biting even while underwater.

A Blue Beauty

If, like Jeff, you're interested in snakes, you'll *love* his next discovery: Florida's

> ## JEFF'S JOURNAL
> ### ON WATER MOCCASINS' DEFENSES
> "When he is frightened, he sort of coils up, pulls the head in, knocks his mouth back, and anything that's going to come trampling him will say, 'Whoa, I gotta stop.' Because his first line of defense is actually camouflage. . . . He melts right in, a master at blending in!"

eastern indigo snake. The largest nonvenomous snake in North America, this purple serpent is also one of the most beautiful in the world.

With a long body and narrow head, the eastern indigo snake is a member of the *Colubridae* family of snakes, one of the largest groups of serpents. And

Science Note

• The eastern indigo snake can grow to be more than 100 inches — or more than 8 feet — long.

• The snake's name comes from its purple-blue, or indigo, shade. The eastern indigo snake has an iridescent shine on its scales.

• The animals' habitat ranges from dry, sandy areas to swamps and ponds.

• Because of habitat loss and other environmental issues, eastern indigo snakes are an endangered species and are protected by law.

Experience Extra: Pop Quiz!

Like other snakes, the eastern indigo snake breeds in the spring and summer. True or false?

(False! Eastern indigos breed in November, while other snakes are beginning to hibernate!)

these serpents are big eaters. They will eat small mammals, toads, frogs, and other amphibians, and snakes, including poisonous coral snakes. (Eastern indigo snakes are immune to coral snake venom.) The animal eats its prey live and headfirst. It does not constrict or poison its prey with venom. Rather, it opens wide and swallows!

Skinks

Skinks are the largest family of lizards, with more than 1,300 skink species in the world. The skinks of Florida are smooth-scaled, shiny animals with an

---

Science Note

• Most skinks are about 6 inches long, though different species range from 5 to 13 inches long.

• Florida skinks have short legs and round tails. Some species have no legs.

• Skinks are usually active during the day.

• When moving fast, some skinks slither from side to side on their bellies, rather than run.

• Skinks are able to shed their tails when they are in defensive mode. The tail begins to grow back in a few weeks.

---

incredible ability: They can regrow a tail or limb if it breaks off.

Alligators vs. Crocodiles

Florida's Everglades National Park is the only place in the world where you can find alligators living alongside crocodiles. Both animals are members of a group called crocodilians. So how can you tell the difference between two of North America's largest reptiles? Well, both alligators and crocodiles have large, powerful jaws. However, alligators have rounded, blunt snouts, and crocodiles have long, tapered snouts. While both top and bottom teeth are visible on crocodiles when their mouths are closed, alligators show only the teeth on their upper jaw when their mouths are closed.

In addition to their physical traits, there is one

Science Note

- Both species can grow to be more than 10 feet long and weigh as much as 1,000 pounds.

- American alligators are grayish black, while American crocodiles are usually tan or olive-brown.

- Both species have large, muscular tails that help the animals move through water and serve as an excellent defense weapon against predators.

- Alligators nest on a mound of vegetation, while crocodiles make nests in mud or sand.

other major difference that separates these reptiles. Crocodiles have adapted to survive in a marine environment and are found near salt water all over the world. Alligators, however, prefer a freshwater environment. But the American crocodile is unique in that it can survive in the freshwater environment of the Everglades.

Now you might think that the number one defense for an alligator is its teeth — and you'd be right. But coming in a close second is the alligator's tail. Alligators have very muscular tails, and when they feel threatened they will curl their tails back and then whip them forward. An alligator's tail is strong enough to break a human's legs. In addition, alligators have very thick hides

Experience Extra:
Pop Quiz!

An alligator constantly grows new teeth, producing upward of 3,000 teeth over the course of its lifetime. True or false?

(True!)

JEFF'S JOURNAL
ON MEETING A HUGE FLORIDA ALLIGATOR

"You can't come to Florida without seeing a gator. This guy is pushing near 14 feet ... weighing somewhere between 800 and 1,000 pounds. It is a perfectly designed animal. Essentially, one great, scaly, eating machine."

covered with bony plates called scutes. These also help to protect the animal from potential predators.

The Panthers of Florida

About 30 different species of mountain lions, or cougars, live in the Western Hemisphere. One of the rarest of all wildcats is the beautiful Florida panther that lives only in subtropical forests and swamp areas in Florida. Once hunted extensively but now protected by law, only about 60 of these amazing animals still live in the wild.

Panthers are usually quiet, but they do communicate through a variety of sounds such as chirps, whistles, purrs, moans, screams, growls, and hisses. When frightened, kittens emit a series of short, high-pitched peeps, and kittens and their mothers keep track of each other with whistles.

Male panthers have large, well-defined home

Science Note

- The Florida panther has short, reddish-gray fur and a broad skull and nose.

- Because there are so few Florida panthers, their gene pool is limited. Members of the species now have distinctive cowlicks on their backs and kinks at the end of their tails as a result of inbreeding.

- Mountain lions are 3 to 4 feet long, stand 25 to 30 inches tall at the shoulder, have long tails, and weigh between 70 and 170 pounds. Though very similar in appearance and closely related to mountain lions, Florida panthers are a smaller species and weigh about 25 percent less than mountain lions.

- These carnivores prey on a variety of animals, including deer, wild hogs, rodents, rabbits, birds, and, on rare occasions, alligators.

ranges that can be about 200 square miles. Female panthers have much smaller ranges, but they require lots of food in that area— especially when they are raising kittens. As more and more people move into the panthers' environment, it is becoming harder for panthers to find a territory. However, conservation efforts are under way to save this unique animal.

From a huge marine creature once mistaken for a mermaid to lizards able to remove — and replace —

their tails, from giant reptiles to one of the rarest cats on Earth, Florida is home to extraordinary animals — and an amazing experience. But our journey isn't over yet.

How much can you recall about the animals of North America? Turn the page to find out!

Experience Quiz:

WILD IN THE U.S.A.

Hey there, fearless experience seekers! Now that you've completed the tremendous trip to some of North America's most fascinating regions, why not test your knowledge of its amazing animals? Try this quick quiz!

1. The Couch's spadefoot toad lives in
a. swamps.
b. deserts.
c. rocky regions.

2. An adult Alaskan moose can weigh as much as
a. 1,600 pounds.
b. 2,000 pounds.
c. 2,400 pounds.

3. Armadillos eat
a. flowers.
b. insects.
c. birds.

4. Alligators do *not* have
a. long, sharp snouts.
b. powerful tails.
c. grayish-black skin.

5. Manatees are related to
a. squids.
b. flounders.
c. elephants.

6. The most venomous snake in North America is
a. the gopher snake.
b. the Mojave rattlesnake.
c. the Arizona long-nosed snake.

7. Alaska is twice the size of
a. California.
b. New York.
c. Texas.

8. Like kangaroos, opossums are
a. marsupials.
b. arachnids.
c. cantankerous.

9. Hooved animals are called
a. unguents.
b. ungulates.
c. uncledates.

10. Unlike seals, sea lions
a. are part of the pinniped family.
b. have external ears.
c. eat fish.

Answers: 1.b, 2.a, 3.b, 4.a, 5.c, 6.b, 7.c, 8.a, 9.b, 10.b.

GLOSSARY

Antidote [AN-tih-doht]: a remedy to counteract the effects of poison.

Antivenin [AN-tih-veh-nuhn]: an antidote for venom.

Aposematic [A-puh-sih-ma-tik]: a word describing coloration or another sign that indicates to others an animal is dangerous.

Arid [AIR-uhd]: dry.

Carnivore [KAHR-nuh-vohr]: meat eater.

Carrion [KAIR-ee-uhn]: dead and rotting flesh.

Cloven [KLOH-vuhn]: split, divided.

Colubrid [KAHL-yuh-bruhd]: any of the usually nonvenomous snakes of the family *Colubridae,* which includes king snakes, garter snakes, and water snakes.

Culvert [KUHL-vert]: a drain or channel.

Descendants [dih-SEHN-duhnts]: offspring of a certain ancestor.

GLOSSARY

Herbivore [UHR-buh-vohr]: plant eater.

Invertebrates [ihn-VUHR-tuh-bruhts]: group of animals that do not have a backbone.

Keen [KEEN]: sharp.

Keratin [KAIR-uh-tuhn]: the material that makes up human fingernails (and rattlesnake rattles).

Marsupials [mahr-SOO-pee-uhls]: a group of mammals in which females carry their young in a pouch.

Musk [MUHSK]: a strong-smelling substance that some animals produce.

Nocturnal [nahk-TUHR-nuhl]: active at night.

Omnivorous [ahm-NIH-vuh-ruhs]: eating any sort of food.

Predator [PREH-duh-tuhr]: an animal that hunts another.

Prehensile [pree-HEHN-suhl]: grasping.

Prey [PRAY]: an animal that is hunted by another.

GLOSSARY

Toxic [TAHK-sihk]: poisonous.

Ungulate [UHN-gyuh-luht]: hooved animal.

Venom [VEH-nuhm]: poison produced by some snakes, insects, and spiders.

Vertebrates [VUHR-tuh-bruhts]: group of animals that have a backbone.

Don't miss any of the experience:

Animal Planet #1: Snakes: Face-to-Face

Did you know that there are over 2,000 different species of snakes? It's true. And here's your chance to meet some of them. Join Jeff Corwin for a trip around the world as he searches for as many of these reptiles as he can find. Be there as Jeff comes face-to-face with cobras, rattlesnakes, sea kraits, and the highly venomous — not to mention aggressive — black mamba. Jeff's caught them all and he's going to share the experience with you.

Animal Planet #2: Into the Rain Forest

This time Jeff Corwin is heading to South America. He's about to have another great experience exploring four different South American destinations and the wildlife that live there. From the eyelash vipers and sloths in Panama to the kinkajous and caiman in Ecuador, the howler monkeys and anacondas in Brazil, and the iguanas and giant tortoises of the Galapagos Islands, it's an experience unlike any other.

Animal Planet #3: Monkeying Around

Join Jeff Corwin as he travels the globe searching for all kinds of primates, like orangutans, howler monkeys, aye-ayes, gibbons, and tiny lemurs. But that's not all, because wherever Jeff goes, he finds lots of other unusual animals and this experience is no different. So he's also going to introduce you to bats, chameleons, and even real dragons!

These books are packed with cool facts and Jeff's own thoughts about the animals he encounters, so you won't want to miss a minute of the experience!